LOW FLYING RABBITS

When he's not writing stories and poems, **Roger Stevens** visits schools and libraries, where he performs his work and helps children and teachers to write and learn more about poetry. His award-winning website, www.poetryzone.co.uk, features work by children from all across the world. Roger used to live at the seaside with his pet rabbit, Ron. They could often be seen strolling along the prom together. Alas, Roger now sits on the beach writing poems alone. Ron was last seen flying his biplane across the Channel towards the coast of France . . .

Nathan Reed lives in South London, where he illustrates from his home studio which he shares with his collection of robots and vinyl rabbits (he's never seen them flying . . . yet!).

Much to his wife Louise's concern, they keep him company during the day while she is doing a proper job!

When he's not conjuring up new characters, Nathan can be found playing tennis or football, although he has acquired a nervous disposition since being made aware of *Low Flying Rabbits*!

Also by Roger Stevens

Why Otters Don't Wear Socks
Poems by Roger Stevens

The Monster That Ate the Universe
Poems by Roger Stevens

The Jumble Book
Poems chosen by Roger Stevens

Poems by
Roger Stevens

Illustrated by Nathan Reed

MACMILLAN CHILDREN'S BOOKS

For Lily, Ruby, Merlin and Sam

First published 2011 by Macmillan Children's Books
a division of Macmillan Publishers Limited
20 New Wharf Road, London N1 9RR
Basingstoke and Oxford
Associated companies throughout the world
www.panmacmillan.com

ISBN 978-0-230-75190-3

Text copyright © Roger Stevens 2011
Illustrations copyright © Nathan Reed 2011

The right of Roger Stevens and Nathan Reed to be identified as the
author and illustrator of this work has been asserted by them in
accordance with the Copyright, Designs and Patents Act 1988.

1 3 5 7 9 8 6 4 2

A CIP catalogue record for this book is available from
the British Library.

Contents

Are You Famous?

On a scale of one to Wordsworth
I am probably a seven
On a scale of soft to very loud
I'm probably eleven
On a scale of one to Einstein
I'm probably one and a half
On a scale of groan to hysteria
I'm probably a laugh
On a scale of one to infinity
I'm a meagre sixty-one
On a scale of A to Z
I hover at F for Fun
On a scale of amoeba to gorilla
I'm sitting on top of the tree
On the scale of now till the end of time
I'm an H for history

Low Flying Rabbits Ahead

Watch out for obstreperous elephants
Or fidgety fleas in your bed
There's a bear on your chair – don't stare!
   Beware!
Low flying rabbits ahead

Be warned! Argumentative aardvarks
And the tigers haven't been fed
When in doubt you must shout, There be
   dragons, watch out!
Low flying rabbits ahead

Caution – cantankerous catfish
There's a dodo called Fred in the shed
And the mad fortune teller says, Take your
    umbrella
Low flying rabbits ahead

Be prepared for the lemur's cruel laughter
Don't forget what the old tortoise said
Life is fun. When in doubt – don't worry about
Those low flying rabbits ahead

Suspense Haiku

It's unexpected.
Midnight. A knock on the door.
You open it. Oh . . .

A Poem That Begins Small

In the beginning was nothing at all
Not even words like these
No trees, no birds, no flowers, no fields,
No land, no fish, no seas

There weren't any people to marvel at things
There was no life at all
And the whole of the all of the vast universe
Was the size of a ping-pong ball

There was so much stuff (a universe worth)
Compressed in that tiny place
That it all went BANG and the BANG was BIG
And it spread to fill up space

And from all that stuff expanding in space
There gradually formed great suns
And from the debris there grew planets and moons
And on one planet, Earth, life began

From a strange concoction of chemicals
From a lightning storm's spark and fizz
And it's why we can gaze in awe at the sky
And write down poems like this

The Hedgehog and the Sloth

I wandered lonely as a hedgehog
Who saunters through the undergrowth
When all at once I met a frog
In conversation with a sloth

You move so slowly, said the frog
You're almost at a stop
But there's so much to do and see
I'm always on the hop

Well, said the sloth, and minutes passed
As the sloth chewed on his lip
The frog waited impatiently
And then said, Toodle pip!

So, said the sloth, eventually,
My views I guess you seek
Then thought some more (about half an hour)
Please come back Thursday week

By now, of course, the frog had gone
To chase a dragonfly
And I resumed my wandering
And ate my custard pie

Branch

There's a branch
Of a tree
That I see
From my window

Horizontal
A thick pencil mark
Across a tiny rectangle
Of sky

And on it sits a bird
Sometimes a crow
Black and sinister
Sometimes a pigeon

The pigeon is fat
Probably the only fat bird
On the estate
With its own private store
Of peanuts

Sometimes I see the pigeon
Sometimes the crow

As I lie in bed
In the morning half awake
Before I open my eyes
I sometimes wonder

Will I see the pigeon
Will I see the crow
Or will the branch be empty?

Marmite or Marmalade?

Mum says,
What would you like for breakfast?
And I say, toast.
Mum says,
What would you like on your toast?
And I say, marmalade.
Mum says,
We've run out of marmalade.
How about strawberry jam?
I say, but I only like marmalade.
We've got raspberry jam.
But I only like marmalade.
Blackcurrant jam? You like that.
Marmalade.
Marmite! You like that.
Marmalade.
Marmite.
Marmalade.
Marmite.
Marmalade.

Look, I can probably just scrape enough
Marmalade from the bottom of the jar.
OK, I'll have Marmite then.
Look, there's just enough marmalade.
I'll have Marmite.
Marmalade.
Marmite.
Marmalade.
Marmite.
Marmalade!
Have we got any cornflakes?

What Was on the Menu?

You wake in the night
And the plan
Is laid out on the tablecloth of your mind
Like a feast
And you know beyond doubt
(And you could swear on your gerbil's grave)
That in the morning when you wake
You'll remember every course, the soup
The sausage pie, the strawberries

But in the morning, when you wake
Yes, you can still taste the food
But you can't begin to remember
You have no idea . . .
What exactly was on the menu

WaSp

A wasp finds itself
Trapped inside my shirt
Escapes without harm

How Can I Be Lonely?

We're a family of eleven
And nearly everyone wants to play
So how can I possibly be lonely?
I ask myself each day

Mum works in the City of London
And Dad is a football scout
But that still leaves eight (not counting me)
So there's always someone about

Our cats Alpha and Beta
They like a bit of fun
Chasing birds around the beanpoles
Or shadows in the sun

And our goldfish Zap and Trevor
You'll never meet fish nicer
I can watch them swim round and round for
    hours
First one way then verse vicer

Harry the hamster's quite funny
With his death-defying tricks
And Judy, our dog, doesn't say very much
But she's brilliant at bringing back sticks

You can chat with Peter the budgie
He'll discuss football, the Villa or Man U
He can talk the hind legs off a python
He can talk till his face turns blue

We're a family of eleven
And nearly everyone wants to play
So how can I possibly be lonely?
I ask myself each day

Oh, I nearly forgot – that's only ten
I've not mentioned my very best mate
If ever, by chance, I do get lonely
I chat to the garden gate

Bounder

The dog is bounding for joy
across the field.
Stops

dead. That dream again.
Where the giant rabbit
leaps
from the rabbit hole

Hello Mum I'm on the Bus

Hello, Mum
Yes, I'm on the bus
No, I'm fine
I left my homework behind. Could you . . .
Yes, I know it was a silly thing to do
So could you . . .
Yes, I am forgetful . . .
Yes, luckily it is screwed on
Anyway, could you . . .
It's on my desk, next to . . .
I know I should have made my bed . . .
Yes, it is in a bit of a mess . . .
I know . . .
I was in a hurry because I overslept . . .
Yes, I should have gone to bed earlier
But I was doing my homework
Anyway, about my homework . . .
Could you bring it to the . . .
OK, I'll tidy my room tonight. Mum?
Could you . . .
We're here now. I've got to get off
I'm at the school
About my homework. Don't bother
I'll say the armadillo ate it again
Bye, Mum

Granny Said a Wise Thing

Granny said a wise thing
when we were quite young.
Granny, that's my mum's mum,
lived across town half a mile away
unlike Dad's mum, who lived next door
in Bleak House
named after Charles Dickens's book,
the writer who wrote *Oliver*
which became a musical –
remember, we saw it in the village hall
but the piano was out of tune
and had been since Mr Dupree died.
And Mr Dupree wasn't French like everyone
    thought
but was born in Doddington
but he *was* blind
and was *never* captured by aliens
and taken on a tour of the universe,
he just made that up,
like he made up his name,
anyway, as Granny once said, very wisely . . .
Now what did she say? I've forgotten.

Brave

When Dad and Mum cannot agree
And I am on my own again
I sit beneath this twisted tree
And shelter from the rain

The sky is black, the lightning white
The weather misbehaves
I wonder, Are birds scared of thunder?
And if so, are they brave?

Friends Like Mine

Jade's mum plays sudoku
Ben's mum walks the Fells
India's mum does dressmaking
My mum yells

Jade's dad just loves crosswords
Ben's dad works with wood
India's dad reads poetry
My dad's in a mood

Jade's folks enjoy board games
Ben's folks ride their bikes
India's folks love cinema
My folks fight

My teacher says my life's my own
And I mustn't be afraid
I'll grow up fine with friends like mine
India, Ben and Jade

Shouting at the Ocean

There's no point shouting at the ocean
When you're feeling low
The tide will still come in
It doesn't want to know

It's no good shouting at the ocean
Just because it's there
You can yell, throw stones or kick the sand
The ocean doesn't care

There's no use railing at the ocean
If you're angry or upset
The sea won't even notice you
It's too busy being wet

For the sea has no emotion
It doesn't hear you shout
It only listens to the moon
It just comes in and out

So if you're hurt, upset or angry
Write down all you want to say
Then post it in the ocean
Watch your troubles float away

The Walking Bus

(Spoken to a Bo Diddley beat)

Come on everybody and walk with us
Yeah, the walking bus
We're walking to school and we don't make a
    fuss
Yeah, the walking bus

At the front Sam holds up a number eight
Yeah, the walking bus
And the walking bus is never late
Yeah, the walking bus

Hold out your hand if you want us to stop
Yeah, the walking bus
Show us your ticket and on you hop
Yeah, the walking bus

Ron is crying and having his airs
Yeah, the walking bus
Cos teacher won't let him go upstairs
Yeah, the walking bus

Sometimes we're slow, sometimes we're fast
Yeah, the walking bus
Sometimes we don't stop, we just walk past
Yeah, the walking bus

Come on everybody and walk with us
Yeah, the walking bus
We're walking to school and we don't make a
    fuss
Yeah, the walking bus

Teacher, Teacher

Teacher, teacher
If you can't find Sue
She's in the cloakroom
Looking for her shoe

Teacher, teacher
If you can't find Ben
He's in with the Head
Cos he's late again

Teacher, teacher
If you can't find Hans
He's still in the shower
Cos he's lost his pants

We Are The Cool

We're Year Six boys
And we are The Cool
The coolest class
In the school

We don't smile
We don't make a fuss
There's no one as cool
As cool as us

We stand in the playground
We talk about stuff
We walk very slowly
Because we are tough

We saunter, we hang
We are nobody's fool
We're the boys in Year Six
And we are The Cool

Change of Position

I had been standing on my teacher's two feet
For some time
When she remarked –
Stand on your own two feet
For once!

Year Six Sisters

We are the Year Six Girls
We are the Year Six Crowd
We are the Year Six Posse
We are the Girls Out Loud

We are the Year Six Sisters
And we know how to have a laugh
We scare the Year Six boys for sure
And they don't dare cross our path

The teachers say we're a dream to teach
But they haven't got a clue
In lessons we're quiet and well behaved
If only the teachers knew

That we're passing notes and swapping jokes
And discussing various ploys
To humiliate and aggravate
And generally wind up the boys

We are the Year Six Posse
The girls of intellect
We are the Year Six Sisters
So treat us with respect

Lessons at the School for Hypnotists

Period eight
Counting backwards
Period seven
Being sleepy
Period six
Being very sleepy
Period five
Your eyes are feeling heavy
Period four
Very, very heavy
Period three
You are asleep
Period two
You are a chicken
Period one
When I click my fingers you will wake up

Humpty Dumpty

Humpty Dumpty
Pole-vaulted the wall
But Humpty Dumpty
Didn't fall

He sailed over
He landed true
And broke the record!
So – naaaghhh to you!

How Miss Broke Her Arm

I heard that . . .
She was ice-skating in Switzerland
And tried to go much faster
Than the speed at which her skates would skate
And now her arm's in plaster

I heard that . . .
She was climbing up a mountain
On the Isle of Thanet
And at the summit was attacked
By an angry black-billed gannet

I heard that . . .
She came across the TARDIS
Became the Doctor's sidekick
Then saved the Earth but caught an errant
Death ray from a Dalek

I heard that . . .
She was captured by a UFO
And taken into space
And a very clever copy
Was left in teacher's place

But the truth is very boring
Mr Blueberry explained it
She stirred a cup of tea too fast
And accidentally sprained it

Sponsored Silence

We said, Let's hold a sponsored swim
Let's hold a sponsored spell
A sponsored clap
A sponsored rap
A sponsored shout and yell

Teacher said, They're great ideas
But they might provoke a riot
Too much noise
So, girls and boys,
Let's hold a sponsored q-u-i-e-t

We said, We understand your fears
We know just what you mean
So we held a vote
And the clear result
Was to a hold a sponsored

How Does It Feel to Be a Poet?

Sometimes it feels fizzy
Like a shaken Coke
Sometimes it's a giggle
Like a naughty joke
Sometimes it feels bouncy
Like a double bed
Sometimes it's surprising
Like a chocolate egg
Sometimes it's the colour blue
Like a sky's hooray
Sometimes it feels slightly sad
Like an upturned day
Sometimes it's underwhelming
Like unbuttered bread
Sometimes it's disappointing
Like mixing green and red
Sometimes it's a worry
Like a dog with fleas
But mostly it's exhilarating
Like a hive of rhyming bees
And it's crazy and amazing
And it's funny and it's mad
It's a party. It's your birthday
The best you ever had

Jack and Jill

Jack and Jill went up the hill
To fetch a pail of water
Jack fell down and broke his crown
And Jill came tumbling after

Up Jack got and home did trot
As fast as he could caper
He went to bed to mend his head
With vinegar and brown paper

Jill was found still on the ground
By her Uncle Charlie
He took her back home to his shack
And fed her eggs and barley

It came to naught, said Jill, distraught
Oh why did my legs falter?
Said Charlie – Oh, did you not know
A tap turns on the water?

Meanwhile poor Jack (still on his back)
Was feeling proper poorly.
Said Doctor Green, Why, Germolene
Would work much better, surely?

Alas, alack, now poor old Jack
To death was soon succumbing
Jill said, said she, If only we
Had known about the plumbing

A Quiet Poem

It's all right
To be quiet
Just to sit
Sit and think
In the quiet
Of the day
It's OK
To be still
Still and quiet
Be as quiet
As the snow
As a cloud
In the sky
As a key
In a lock

As the tick
(tick)
As the tock
(tock)
(tick)
(tock)
Of a grandfather clock
Just to sit
In the quiet
Of the day
Or the night
It's all right
To be quiet

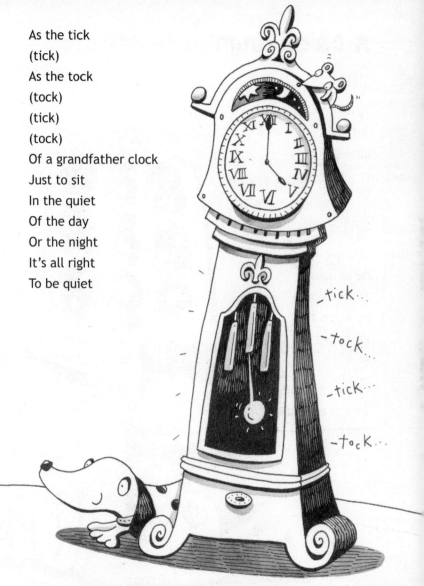

-tick...
-tock...
-tick...
-tock...

*(When this poem is read aloud everyone
repeats each line . . . very quietly)*

My Amazing Poem-Writing Pen

(For Shel Silverstein)

This is the pen I use for writing poems
It wrote some classics –
'The Iguana with the Invisible Tail'
'Beware! Low Flying Rabbits'
'Don't Tell Mum She's Got a Big Bum'
(To name but three . . .)

And what's more
It wrote *this* poem
I bet you'd like a pen like this!

It can rhyme, chime,
Alliterate amazingly
Keep time in four four or six eight
It's a dab hand at metaphor

And what's more
This amazing poem-writing pen belongs to me

It's not available in the shops

I bet you'd like a pen like this
Wouldn't you?

Then take it
It's yours

Take it
A gift

Go on

Now write me a poem

Short-Sleeved Shirt and Shorts

(To be read out loud)

Oh, I'd love to be a sailor
Sailing into sunny ports
I'd sip my sherbet in the shade
In my short-sleeved shirt and shorts

Short-sleeved shirt and shorts
Short-sleeved shirt and shorts
I'd sip my sherbet in the shade
In my short-sleeved shirt and shorts

It's the summer holidays
And I'm on the tennis courts
Knocking the tennis ball about
In my short-sleeved shirt and shorts

Short-sleeved shirt and shorts
Short-sleeved shirt and shorts
Knocking the tennis ball about
In my short-sleeved shirt and shorts

How soon the summer slips away
And school's back in my thoughts
Back to long-sleeved shirt and trousers
No more short-sleeved shirt and shorts

Short-sleeved shirt and shorts
Short-sleeved shirt and shorts
Back to long-sleeved shirt and trousers
No more short-sleeved shirt and shorts

Deceptive

I like the fact that
Poems can be deceptive
You think you're reading
A free-form ramble
Then you discover that it's
A pair of haikus

Likewise
Discovering that a poem
Is in fact a cinquain
Stood on its head
For fun

Fable

At writing Aesop was tip-top
But his limericks, alas, weren't much cop
His first lines were fine
And his rhymes were divine
But he just didn't know when to stop
And always wrote a little moral on the end

A Week of Haikus

1
At Clapham Junction
The carriage lurches forward
Crumbs on the seat

2
What's the meaning of
Antidisestablishmentarianism?

3
Clouds edge the horizon
The boat is two hours late
Heavy scent of thyme

4
Beware nettles and
Overenthusiastic
Thistles. And brambles

5
Sit, sit, sit, dog, sit
Good boy, sit, go on, sit, sit
Sit, sit, sit, sit, please . . .

6
Around the corner
Sweep five sleek black limousines
Moosh, spelt in flowers

7
The long holiday
A patch of sunlight creeping
Slowly round the bed

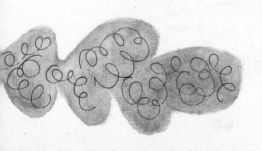

I Wish

I wish I were an *
I wouldn't be for show
I'd add important information
When you looked **

* asterisk
** below

46

Not Arial, Not Times Roman

If I could invent
A font
I would call it
All Knowledge

Metaphor Poem

He is a sentence, its words chosen for their own sake
He is an ancient arrowhead, caked with Saxon mud
A visit to the soothsayer who is slow on the uptake
His words are lightly written in anything but blood
He is a tune heard faintly in the early afternoon
A sprinter running for the Gatwick Express
A sprig of bracken, a branch of broom
A grass snake hovering on the edge
A drawer made out of yellow plastic
On Gothic moors – a swirling mist
He's a mean zero, he is elastic
A mermaid's secret salty kiss
The son of a saucepan lid
A gold and silver seam
A World-Cup bid
He's a dream

A Let-Down

Cinquains
Can disappoint
They start promisingly
As each line grows, tension builds, then
They end

untidy Poem

What an untiy pome

It's a DISGRICE
leTTers anD words
all over the place

No oNe will lke it
they won't even

LOOK

It will never get publisid
in a P

PoetrY BOOK

How Long Does It Take to Write a Poem?

I'm not yet sure
Let me check the time
It's seven minutes to ten
And thirty-two seconds
It's Sunday morning
And I'm peering out of the window
At the cars rushing along the Vauxhall Bridge
    Road
Wondering what to write next
Two minutes thirty-five seconds so far
Of course there will be a redrafting, maybe two
And there's the possibility that this may never
    become a poem
Just a few scribbled lines in my notebook
And when the notebook is full
It will sit on the old notebook shelf
With all the other old notebooks
Waiting for a day that may never come
When Indiana Jones finds the room's hidden
    entrance
In the rubble and the rocks
Blows the dust from the book's cover
Opens it and begins to read
How long does it take to write a poem?
Eight minutes, twenty-three seconds

Price List

For fun verse
Shrieks and hollers
$20

For lyrical flights
That know no bounds
£20

For passionate prose
At Uncle Joe's
€20

For light verse and nonsense
That's less intense
20 pence

To write a poem
With me
Free

The Old Royal Observatory, Greenwich

You need time to see
All there is to see
At the Old Royal Observatory

In the octagonal room
The long pendulum of time
Swings slowly

And on a cool New Year's Eve
You found yourself
Standing on the frost-flecked slopes

Of Observatory Hill
Watching for the second
Which every year escapes

But the new-fangled atomic clock
Loses only one second
Every billion years

And you find yourself wondering
How did we live
With such a gaping margin of error?

Poem for Choosing a Holiday Destination

We could photograph lions
On the African plain
Watch as they stalk the okapi
We could go to Bombay
For a real takeaway
Or Oz for a genuine barbie

We could go to Hawaii
And ride on the surf
Or sail on a luxury liner
Be amazed at the view
From the top of St Paul's
Or climb the Great Wall of China

We could dive in the deep
Where the sea monsters sleep
Swim with dolphins and wave to the whales
Go white-water rafting
In Peru and Brazil
And follow the mountainous trails

But who wants to explore
The chateaux of France?
Why hanker for castles in Spain?
How we cheered when Mum said
Our account's in the red
So we're going to Margate again

Unlucky You

Travelling by car is much more fun
Than flying in an aeroplane
Anyway, Mum gets airsick
And there's nothing to see when you're up in the
    clouds

I'm glad we didn't go to Italy
Because I can't speak Italian
And Margate beach is underrated
When it rains the glistening sands are beautiful

In Italy, Alex says, the sound of the surf
Keeps you awake
But we're not far from the beach
It's only a ten-minute walk, if you run

You don't see many dolphins from Margate beach
But, even better, we swam with the jellyfish
We much prefer fish and chips
Who wants to eat boring old spaghetti Bolognese
   anyway?

I'm glad we went to Margate
Not to Italy, like my best mate Alex
Mum said we mustn't tell him what a great time
   we had
He'll only be jealous

Announcement

This is my favourite
Announcement
On the London Underground
Northern Line

This station
Is Oval

-MIND THE GAP -

Manchester to Euston

Squeezed into the tube of train we rumble
Through the night, decelerate and stop
At Milton Keynes, an icy blast of air
Voices scatter and regroup, phones mumble,
Squashed into this can, where men talk shop
We stumble as the train moves on. Beware.
A ring pull frees me from the crush, I tumble
To a place of darkened dreams, I slowly drop
Where songs from moon-blessed nightbirds fill
   the air
And star-blessed foxes feed me custard creams
Where badgers wander through the hedgerows
   musing
And bats betray their vampire-masters' schemes
My legs are cramped, my thoughts are in
   confusion
How pleased I'll be to leave the train at Euston

Visit to Edinburgh

We walk the Royal Mile
To Edinburgh Castle
And the guide tells us
That at the Edinburgh Tattoo
You can see – and hear –
Switzerland's
Top-Secret Drum Corps
Excuse me?
How can you keep
A noise like that secret?

Rooks

Do the thousand roosting rooks
Have to say goodnight
To *every* member
Of their family
Before they turn in?

The Death's-Head Hawkmoth

Twilight deepens
In the graveyard
And the first cicadas sing

Moth's quick shadow
On the gravestone
Human skull between its wings

The moth's soft touch
Against your cheekbone
Fear is such a fragile thing

The harbinger
Glimpsed by moonlight
Human skull between its wings

Snail Race

To organize a snail race

Draw a starting line
On the path
In chalk

Place a lettuce leaf
One pace away

Show two snails the lettuce
Then place them on the line

Say,
'On your marks, get set,
Go!'

Prepare to be bored

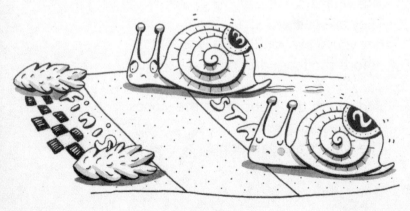

The Boy Who Cried Wolf

You can watch the sky
And the wind patterning the grass
And try to understand the ways of sheep
But you'll get bored
In the end
Or fall asleep

Wolf! You cry out
You blow your whistle, ring your bell
Call the wolf hotline on your mobile phone
And the villagers come
But there is no wolf

Later, you try it again
This time making it sound more urgent
Come quickly. The wolf has carried off a
     newborn lamb!
The villagers come
They are angry. You are sorry
But you know you'll do it again
Before the long, dreary day is through

And where the trees meet the slopes
As the evening fades
The wolves are gathering

Natural Breaks

1
The sun is barely up
Cross-hatching, scratched into icy fields
Dazzles like the sky

2
A tree
Bereft of leaves
Caught, frozen in position
Running across a field

Lesser-Known Children's Games

Scribble
Tease the Tiger
Throw the Worm Over the Wall
Shout Monkey!
Who's Hidden Harriet?
How Far Can You Fall?

Hop Irish
Skip Welsh
Jump Over the Moat
Chase the Goldfish
Hurl the Spoon
Put the Coat on the Stoat

Last One Up the Chimney Is a Sooty Beggar
Turnip Ball
Kiss the Rat
Snakes and Larders
Pancake Frisbee
Put the Hat on the Sprat

Today We Beat Brazil

Today we beat Brazil ten-nil
Ten-nil
Ten-nil
Today we beat Brazil ten-nil
And our striker is a dog

The game with Poland was called off
And we were winning
Seven-three
The game with Poland was called off
Cos our striker burst the ball

Tomorrow we play Italy
Italy
Italy
Tomorrow we play Italy
If we can find a ball

We're going to win the World Cup
World Cup
World Cup
We're going to win the World Cup
All we need's a ball

(And a new striker who is not a Border collie)

Fielding

Our captain said, Right! You stand at silly mid-off
I said, OK. But wouldn't it be better
If I stood at very silly mid-off?
Billy said, Why don't you stand
At stupid mid-off?
Our captain said, No!
Just stand at silly mid-off
I said, Could I stand at ridiculous mid-off?
Billy said, Why don't you stand
At pants mid-off?

The umpire, Mr Walton, said,
Just do it – or you'll be on litter duty
So I said, Silly mid-off it is then
Billy said, You could stand at . . .
The umpire, Mr Walton, said,
Billy! That's enough!

Cricket Puzzler

Teacher asked us a cricket quiz
How can a wicketkeeper get you out?
The question
Had me stumped

Head Game

I threw you the red ball
You tossed it aside

I threw you the purple ball
You put it in your pocket

I threw you the yellow ball
You threw it in the fire

You weren't in the mood
For imaginary catching

Passport

To visit my secret world
You need a passport
Which you send for on the Internet
Or you can get special permission
To make your own
As long as they stamp it
With their special gold stamp
Most people fly there
In a Boeing 999
But you can walk
If you know the secret way
I stumbled upon it walking Kenny my dog
There was a gap

Where bits of the world
Don't quite join up
Like that shirt my gran made
And Kenny, looking for a rabbit, found it
And I followed him
The weather?
Very hot and sunny all the time
Although I went in winter once
And it rained non-stop
And when I got home
I told Mum I'd fallen in the pond
What's my secret place called?
Its name is secret
No one knows it
I could take you there if you like
To my World without a Name
You just need your passport

Milly

I fancy Milly
The captain of the girls' cricket team
She's a real catch
She bowls me over
She's got a wicket smile
That creases me up
I want to ask her out
But I don't know how to pitch it
It's got me stumped
She knocks me for six
My love for her knows no boundaries

Fragment of a Poem Found by a Lake

The lake is as calm
As an upturned sky

We sit amidst daisies and buttercups
In dappled willow shade

You are reading a comic
I am writing a poem

A silence startles us
Birds freeze in mid-flight

The lake shimmers
Ripples, churns

A dark shape rises like an upset paint pot
Black on blue sugar-paper

It blots out the sun
The sky is full of hissing

Panic!

Run . . .

Wrap Up Warm

Shouting at the ocean won't stop the tide
   advancing
Railing against the storm will only strain your
   throat
Crying in an empty bed will make the night much
   darker
Love may melt the coldest heart but in winter
   wear a coat

Monday's Child

Monday's child selects
From her white wardrobe
A blue dress

Tuesday's child dances
Across the playground
Heads the ball

Wednesday's child worries
Three more days of maths
And counting

Thursday's child decides
Her map of the world is
Incomplete

Friday's child donates
His Lego to the
Flood Appeal

Saturday's child rises
Early for the best
Market place

Sunday's child chases
The shadows of clouds
On the grass

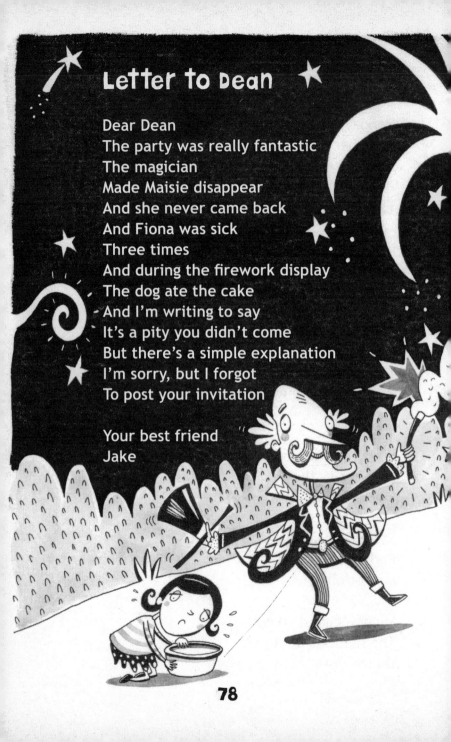

Letter to Dean

Dear Dean
The party was really fantastic
The magician
Made Maisie disappear
And she never came back
And Fiona was sick
Three times
And during the firework display
The dog ate the cake
And I'm writing to say
It's a pity you didn't come
But there's a simple explanation
I'm sorry, but I forgot
To post your invitation

Your best friend
Jake

I Can't See You Any More

Thirteen today
And I'm trying not to cry
But I've just had to wave
My best friend goodbye

She's thirteen, like me
And it doesn't mean
You can't have feelings
If you can't be seen

An invisible friend
Can love just as madly
And invisible tears
Can hurt just as badly

Try Me

I don't do cute
I'll fry you
Just give me the chance
Half a breath will do it
You say you want to study me?
The last surviving dragon
Ha!
Do you think I was born yesterday?
I was born before you could walk on two legs
I was born before you could talk
And I know what you want
Don't deny it
And who says I have any gold anyway?
Just let your defences slip
Just once
Go on
And I'll fry you

The Home for Old Pirates

At the Old Pirates' Rest Home in Bournemouth
Calico Jack has a snooze
He dreams of the Jolly Roger
And a Caribbean cruise

Lafayette Brassoes his buttons
Reliving his fights blow by blow
Long John Silver hunts for his parrot
But his parrot passed on long ago

Blackbeard manoeuvres his Zimmer
Anne Bonny pours rum in her tea
While Captain Hook sits in the window seat
Ears pricked for the tick
Of the crocodile's clock
And stares sadly out to sea

Teacher, Teacher

(Alternative version)

Teacher, teacher
Millicent Witt
Has hidden the hamster
In her PE kit

Teacher, teacher
Jeremy Pear
Has hidden Beth's socks
And he won't tell her where

Teacher, teacher
Alasdair Tup
Says these rhymes are contrived
And the names are made up

My Mother is

My mother is a diamond
An emerald
A pearl
A sapphire
A ruby
She's that kind of girl

An amethyst
A moonstone
A lapis lazuli
My mother rocks!
She is a gem
A precious thing to me

Weightlessness

As the spaceship turns in to the planet's pull
Weightlessness

As the teacher looks up from her book
And sees you just about
To throw the paper dart
Weightlessness

As the sandman drapes
The cape of darkness
On your half-formed thoughts
Weightlessness

Before you are born, when you are gone
Weightlessness

The Most Important Rap

(With thanks to Denis Waitley)

I am an astronaut
I circle the stars
I walk on the moon
I travel to Mars
I'm brave and tall
There is nothing I fear
and I am the most important person here

I am a teacher
I taught you it all
I taught you why
your spaceship doesn't fall
If you couldn't read or write
where would you be?
The most important person here is me

Who are you kidding?
Are you taking the mick?
Who makes you better
when you're feeling sick?
I am a doctor
and I'm always on call
and I am more important than you all

But I am your mother
Don't forget me
If it wasn't for your mother
where would you be?
I washed your nappies
and changed your vest
I'm the most important
and Mummy knows best

I am a child
and the future I see
and there'd be no future
if it wasn't for me
I hold the safety
of the planet in my hand
I'm the most important
and you'd better understand

Now just hold on
I've a message for you all
Together we stand
and divided we fall
So let's make a circle
and all remember this
Who's the most important?
EVERYBODY IS!

Night Sounds

The hoot of an owl
The purr of a car
The thud of a door
The scratch of a key
The click of a lock
The squeak of a hinge
The click of a heel
The creak of the stair
The groan of the floor
The swing of the door
The whisper of draught
The scuff of a shoe
The shiver of breath
The rustle of clothes
The kiss of a kiss
The silence of sleep